SOME SMAL

SOME SMALL HEAVEN

SEEKING LIGHT IN WINTER

ADVENT, CHRISTMAS & EPIPHANY

Ian Adams

CANTERBURY PRESS
Norwich

First published in 2017 by the Canterbury Press Norwich
Editorial office
3rd Floor, Invicta House
108–114 Golden Lane
London EC1Y 0TG, UK

www.canterburypress.co.uk

Canterbury Press is an imprint of Hymns Ancient & Modern Ltd
(a registered charity)

Hymns Ancient & Modern® is a registered trademark of
Hymns Ancient & Modern Ltd
13A Hellesdon Park Road, Norwich,
Norfolk NR6 5DR, UK

British Library Cataloguing in Publication data

A catalogue record for this book is available
from the British Library

978 1 84825 993 5

Printed and bound by CPI Group (UK) Ltd, Croydon, CR0 4YY

CONTENTS

reflections experienced, considered and written in real time

to discover the light within the darkness
of winter – and within all our winters

INTRODUCTION

Winter tests our hope and resolve. In the Northern hemisphere the temperature drops. Storms disturb. Light fades. But this time of year also sees the festivals of Advent, Christmas and Epiphany. Each in some way is a reminder that light is never totally absent. Exploring a path through these festivals, *Some Small Heaven* seeks to discover the light *within* the darkness of winter – and within all our winters – to find *some small heaven* each day, even when life comes at us tough, hard and bleak.

This series of reflections was written each day in real time in Advent, Christmas and Epiphany. As with its predecessor *Wilderness Taunts*, the core of each reflection remains as it was experienced, considered and written at the time. There is darkness, and there is light.

In the South West that winter, as the first reflections for *Some Small Heaven* were being shaped, the weather was challenging. Storm, floods. And such rain! The weather close to horizontal. I was also weathering some personal storms. I have come to know that every year as late autumn slides into winter I am liable to experience sadness. I *feel* the encroaching darkness. Everything out there shapes my inner sense of being. The fallen leaves disintegrating back into earth. The rising water. The gusting wind. My stability is tested.

Such experiences are of course not unusual. You will probably have experienced something similar. So I share these personal reflections knowing that they are part of the human story, and I offer them in the hope that they may be of some gift to the reader.

Advent is particularly associated with waiting. Times of waiting, of course, don't just coincide with the festivals of the Church – and this book can be read and used at any time. But if we can work out how to wait *now*, in this season, we may better understand how to negotiate the waiting times *whenever* they come.

to discover the light within the darkness

Whether we are waiting for a darkness to pass – or yearning for a light to come, the waiting and the yearning deserve our care and our attention.

One of the many gifts of Christmas is its capacity to nurture within us an openness to new possibilities coming into being, unseen, unlikely, unnoticed. Closer than we may imagine, something new is always being birthed. God coming towards us, God with us, God within us. A stream of light under the door of darkness.

The Epiphany – the *revealing* – invites us to look up and to look out. To glimpse wider patterns at work in and beyond our own winter horizons. However difficult things may appear out there right now is not how they will always be. And Epiphany suggests that, whatever our spiritual path or tradition, the holy child Jesus may somehow be a gift for us all. In seeking light we may discover that we too are bearers of light. As the holy child-become-man would one day say to those around him: *You* are the light.

The reflections draw on lines from a series of songs that can be found in the gospel-writer Luke's account of the nativity of Jesus. Luke places these songs at the heart of his narrative, opening up the demands and the wonder of what may be coming into being. There's Mary's song of joy, the wonderful *Magnificat*; Zechariah's prophetic song of possibility, the *Benedictus*; the astonishing *Songs of the Angels* extolling the birth of the holy child Jesus; and there's Simeon's tender song of praise to God, the *Nunc Dimittis*, born out of the holy waiting that he and the prophet Anna had undergone.

The photographs for the book were all taken in winter on the coasts of Devon and Cornwall. A key element in my photography is the nurturing of attention to light. These images reflect my attempts to find light in the darkness of winter, and so each day to discover some small heaven …

Grace and peace to you
Ian

you are the light

A STREET EPIPHANY

On the day you awake in the dark
caught in the gut, in the pit, in the pitch
of some shadow advent,
the breath punched from you
sent heavy as you stumble
then fall, shaken forsaken
remembered no more

May you be caught
by the light
of some small heaven
a street epiphany
settle ember soft
upon you

And upon earth,
peace.

THE MAGNIFICAT (MARY'S SONG)

Luke 1.46–55

And Mary said,

My soul magnifies the Lord,
and my spirit rejoices in God my Saviour,
for he has looked with favour on the lowliness of his servant.
Surely, from now on all generations will call me blessed;
for the Mighty One has done great things for me,
and holy is his name.
His mercy is for those who fear him
from generation to generation.
He has shown strength with his arm;
he has scattered the proud in the thoughts of their hearts.
He has brought down the powerful from their thrones,
and lifted up the lowly;
he has filled the hungry with good things,
and sent the rich away empty.
He has helped his servant Israel,
in remembrance of his mercy,
according to the promise he made to our ancestors,
to Abraham and to his descendants forever.

song of joy

THE BENEDICTUS (ZECHARIAH'S SONG)

Luke 1.67–79

Then [John's] father Zechariah was filled with the Holy Spirit and spoke this prophecy:

Blessed be the Lord God of Israel,
for he has looked with favour on his people and
redeemed them.
He has raised up a mighty saviour for us
in the house of his servant David,
as he spoke through the mouth of his holy prophets
from of old,
that we would be saved from our enemies
and from the hand of all who hate us.
Thus he has shown the mercy promised to our ancestors,
and has remembered his holy covenant,
the oath that he swore to our ancestor Abraham,
to grant us that we, being rescued from the hands of
our enemies,
might serve him without fear, in holiness and righteousness
before him all our days.
And you, child, will be called the prophet of the Most High;
for you will go before the Lord to prepare his ways,
to give knowledge of salvation to his people
by the forgiveness of their sins.
By the tender mercy of our God,
the dawn from on high will break upon us,
to give light to those who sit in darkness and in the shadow
of death,
to guide our feet into the way of peace.

song of possibility

SONGS OF THE ANGELS

Luke 2.10–14

But the angel said to them,

Do not be afraid; for see –
I am bringing you good news of great joy for all the people:
to you is born this day in the city of David a Saviour,
who is the Messiah, the Lord.
This will be a sign for you:
you will find a child wrapped in bands of cloth and lying
in a manger.

And suddenly there was with the angel a multitude of the heavenly host, praising God and saying,

Glory to God in the highest heaven,
and on earth peace among those whom he favours!

astonishing songs

THE NUNC DIMITTIS (SONG OF SIMEON AND ANNA)

Luke 2.29–38

Simeon took [the child Jesus] in his arms and praised God, saying,

Master, now you are dismissing your servant in peace,
according to your word;
for my eyes have seen your salvation,
which you have prepared in the presence of all people,
a light for revelation to the Gentiles
and for glory to your people Israel.

And the child's father and mother were amazed at what was being said about him. Then Simeon blessed them and said to his mother Mary,

This child is destined for the falling and the rising of many in Israel, and to be a sign that will be opposed so that the inner thoughts of many will be revealed – and a sword will pierce your own soul too.

There was also a prophet, Anna the daughter of Phanuel, of the tribe of Asher. She was of a great age, having lived with her husband seven years after her marriage, then as a widow to the age of eighty-four. She never left the temple but worshipped there with fasting and prayer night and day. At that moment she came, and began to praise God and to speak about the child to all who were looking for the redemption of Jerusalem.

tender song

[01] PEACEFUL GROUND

The cruelty and violence of the world triggers, unseen,
a violent response within you.
You want to respond.
To bring fire to fire.
Darkness to darkness.
Take them out.

Do you see how the violence of others
becomes in some way your violence too?
You are implicated.

But you are a person of peace.
With Mary your deepest desire is to love,
always moving towards devotion.

So this Advent, as the embers and ashes of violence swirl,
resolve to become the peaceful ground
on which those embers and ashes may settle,
may lose the heat of their anger, and may burn out.

PRAYER WORD

become peaceful ground

my soul magnifies the Lord

[02] YOUR PEACE FOR A PEACEFUL WORLD

To become peaceful ground
the peace you seek will need to evolve
from an idea into a practice.
From something you advocate, into something *you are.*

Peace in your world
can only come into being in so far as you are peaceful.

Your peace will produce a peaceful world.
Or your anxiety will produce an anxious world,
your fear a fearful world,
and your anger an angry world.

Your peace is not beyond you.
It has always been present,
an element of your divine belonging.

This peace is best rediscovered one moment at a time.

So today, practise the peace that is within you.
Let each decision, each action and each reaction
become an act of peace.
And so you will find that peace is waiting for you.

PRAYER WORD

the peace within you

my spirit rejoices in God my Saviour

[03] RUNNING IN THE DARK

You are running in the dark.
The reflective strips on your shoes are of no help to you.
Barely hinting at a path for any naive enough to follow.

The weather matches your internal spirit.
High winds and rain squalls leaving you disturbed.
Last night you dreamed of pain.
With no means to end it all.

In the valley of shadows you were fearful.
You felt alone.
Was anyone looking on you with favour?

So you keep running.
What else can you do?

And as you run
you sense that the sound of breathing is not yours alone.

PRAYER WORD

not alone

he has looked with favour on the lowliness of his servant

[04] OVERWHELMED, CHOOSE TO LOVE

You can feel overwhelmed by the hate in the world.
By the bitterness.
The cynicism.
And the reversion to shame and blame.
You are fearful for your children
and for their children.
For all children.

You long to bring beauty, hope and healing.
To bless
and to be blessed.
But you can barely bring yourself to leave the room.

As far as you can,
wait for your spirit to rise.

Begin to let the energy of your overwhelming
become a source of goodness.
Choose what you can.
Choose to love.

PRAYER WORD

choose to love

surely, from now on all generations will call me blessed

[05] SOME SMALL HEAVEN

You cannot sleep.
A series of bad dreams and the smallest noises wake you.
Your peaceful dream places are elusive.
The white-walled croft above the beach,
at the foot of the rain-catching mountain
has disappeared.
An illusion.

You cannot think, dream or even pray your way out of this.
So what can you do?

As tired as you are
look for heaven here and now.

Let this moment, this hour, this day
become your peaceful dream place.
Let it become, as it is, a great thing.
some small heaven.

PRAYER WORD

some small heaven

the Mighty One has done great things for me

[06] THE CLARITY YOU SEEK

The clarity you seek is elusive.
The water disturbed.
All cloud, grit and mud. Debris and turbulence.

Flood water rising.
You sense the disturbance reaching into all parts of you.
Your fears and hopes becoming indistinguishable from
each other.

All you can do is remain watchful.
To allow the sediment to sink.
To wait for the water to settle.

Let the water discover its true clarity.
Wait for the light to shine. Allow the holy.

PRAYER WORD

allow the holy

and holy is his name

[07] RETURN TO THE BREATH

Your breathing is hard.
Fast. Erratic. You flail.
A torrent of thoughts
overwhelming the rhythm that is natural to you.

On this demanding day, in a demanding season,
how will you recover your stillness?

Begin with the breath.
Deep, long, slow.
And a pause.

Such mercy.
Each breath a receiving of heaven.
The gift of life.

Then the Lord God formed man from the dust of the ground,
and breathed into his nostrils the breath of life;
*and the man became a living being**.

Return to the breath.

PRAYER WORD

[no words, just your breathing]

---

* Genesis 2

his mercy is for those who fear him from
generation to generation

[08] SPEAK TENDER

*Speak tenderly**, speak comfort.

To speak tenderly to others
first speak tenderly
to yourself.

You can be so harsh towards yourself.
Critical of your decisions and of your indecision.

Trust the strength of the Love that calls you.
The Love that surrounds you.
The Love that follows you.

The tenderness is yours.
To receive and to give.
Today speak tender.

PRAYER WORD

speak tender

* Isaiah 40

he has shown strength with his arm

[09] THE HOPE OF THE FEW

When the powerful manipulate the truth,
when the powerless are exploited,
and when we who seek good seem incapable of bringing change,
where is hope?

Advent is a celebration of the few.
Of the small.
Of the unknown and of the unnoticed.

Never forget the potential
of a prayer made in seclusion,
of one generous action,
of some small gesture of faith,
or of a simple blessing
– to scatter the proud
and to shatter their illusion that theirs is the last word.

As alone as you may feel.
As small, as unknown or as unnoticed.
Your prayers, your generosity, your gestures, and your blessings
will heal the world.

PRAYER WORD

healing the world

he has scattered the proud in the thoughts of their hearts

[10] OUT INTO THE OCEAN

In the waiting time you have decisions to make.
Your thought process of course can be flawed.
Your motives will be mixed.
Your thinking muddy and muddled.

But your deep yearning to be true
is not in doubt.
Faith, hope and love *(the greatest of these)*
are your desire.

To become some small gift to the world
step ever more deeply into your calling.
Let *this* be your decision.

From the mouth of the river
wade out into the ocean.
Swim towards the light.
The ocean will carry you.

PRAYER WORD

towards the light

he has brought down the powerful from their thrones

[11] WHEN THE WAVE THAT IS JOY

When the wave that is joy comes
let it carry you.

The waves that are fear are plentiful
and must be ridden out,
causing you to look back lest you are swamped.

But this season the wave that is joy seems elusive.
It must be watched for.
But it will come.

And when it comes
ride it with boldness.
Let it lift you up.

Look for the wave that is joy.

PRAYER WORD

joy

and lifted up the lowly

[12] LET THE SONG

*They shall return with singing**

Whatever you are going through this Advent
listen for the music.

In darkness and in light
songs offer themselves to you for the singing.
An unknown *Magnificat* of joy.
Some ancient *Benedictus* blessing.
A *Nunc Dimittis* in the new now.
And the barely imagined *Songs of Angels* diminishing fear.

Allow music to surprise you today.
To open you up to new possibilities.
To fill you with the rhythm of good things.
Let the song.

And you shall return with singing.

PRAYER WORD

[the words of your song]

---

* The Canticle: Song of the Wilderness

he has filled the hungry with good things

[13] YOU SHALL FEAR DISASTER NO MORE

*You shall fear disaster no more**

Yet you do fear disaster.
In your own life.
In your family. In the world.
Everything, it seems, is going to hell.
Humanity emptying itself of goodness.
So how shall you fear disaster no more?

This is not about never experiencing disaster.
Experiences of descent, loss and darkness
are part of what it means to be human.
They come your way, and will continue to do so.

It's about choosing not to allow fear to shape you.

Resolve today to choose fear's opposite.
To choose love.
This choice will change you.
And it will change the world around you.

And so you shall fear disaster no more.

PRAYER WORD

choose love

---

* Zephaniah 3

and sent the rich away empty

[14] A SKETCH FOR SOME HEAVENLY THING (ST JOHN OF THE CROSS)

You began this day with such high hopes.
With St John of the Cross your guide and companion
you imagined light, however dark the night.
Now you feel crushed by a day of frustration
and encroaching darkness.
With barely a creative moment.

But as important as your work is to you
beware the temptation to achieve.
For St John the key is to receive.

You are not so much the writer,
as the one being written on.
Written through.
Written in.

Allow yourself to become some small ikon.
The rough draft for a short story.
The spark for a poem.
A sketch for some heavenly thing.
A blessing.
And this will be enough.

PRAYER WORD

A sketch for some heavenly thing

blessed be the Lord God of Israel

[15] AND BE RADIANT

*Look upon him and be radiant**

Where are you looking?

You keep looking down.
And looking back.
As if you are afraid that you may fall.
Or afraid that you have lost something.
Or missed something.

But you are looking in the wrong direction.
Turning in a way that is sending you off balance.

Instead, face forward.
Lift up your head.
Look up.
Look not for something
But look for the *someone* who is alongside you and before you.
The One who is looking upon you.

Look upon him and be radiant.

PRAYER WORD

and be radiant

---

* Psalm 34

for he has looked with favour on his people and
redeemed them

[16] LET THE STORM

The season has already left you feeling jaded.
The weather feeding into your mood.
The challenges you face looming.
Yet another storm of great weight and power.
Your attempts to shore up your battered shoreline
exhausting and ineffective.
Cliffs crumbling.

But you have flood plains.
Move onto the surrounding higher ground,
and let the sea flood in.
Allow the marshlands to do their work.
Let them absorb the storm
and hold the sea
until it is ready to recede.
Your salvation is close.

Let the storm come.

PRAYER WORD

let the storm come

he has raised up a mighty saviour for us

[17] GENEALOGY

You speak out the names at the beginning of
Matthew's Gospel.
Familiar and unusual to your ear.
The family – the house of David – unfolds through
generations.
Abraham, Isaac, Jacob, Judah, Perez and Zerah by Tamar …
Friends and strangers to you.
You've never lingered here before.
But each name – each person – played their part in the
great story.

Remember the people today who
have played their part in *your* being here now.
In your surviving.
In your flourishing.
Give thanks for them.

And resolve to treat your family and your friends,
your neighbour and the stranger
with a tenderness that deepens each day.

May your house be a source of blessing.

PRAYER WORD

source of blessing

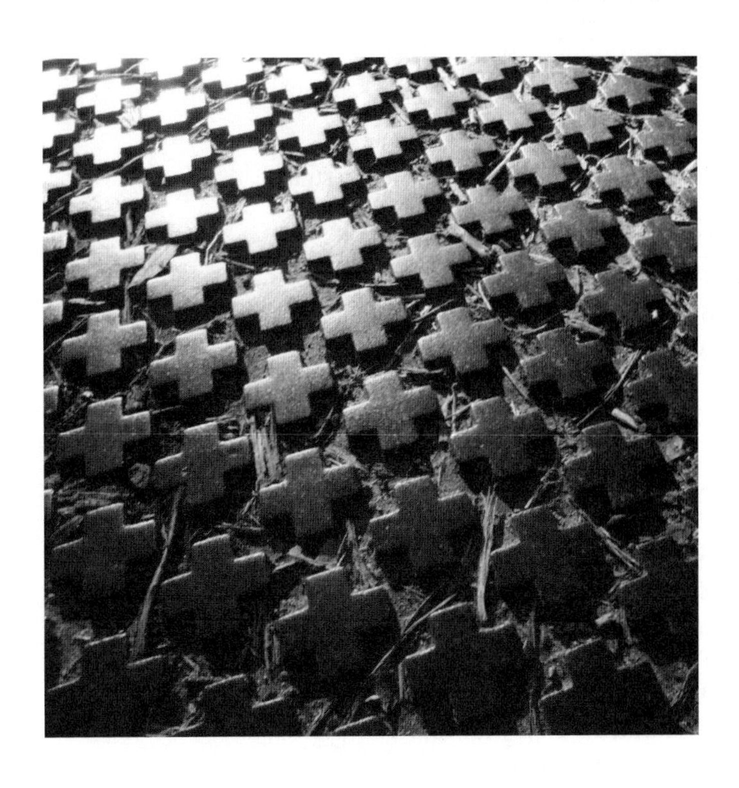

in the house of his servant David

[18] LET THE STORY

The story is so familiar, and yet so strange.
These ancient voices inspire you,
Yet they trouble you too.
The story further complicated now
by all that is going on in the world.
And by all that is going on within you.

Can you let the story of *God with us* find you again?

Allow it to happen around you.
Don't force it.
But when the story finds you
allow yourself to find your place within it.

The story is also your story.
Become the person it is calling into being.
God with us. God with you. You with God.
Let the story find you.

PRAYER WORD

God with us

as he spoke through the mouth of his holy prophets
from of old

[19] THE HOPE OF ANGELS

Zechariah was struck dumb.
The consequence, the story goes, of his inability to believe the angel.

When we ignore the angels of holy possibility
we lose the ability to speak hope and salvation
into a demanding world.

You lean into the great story each day.
It supports the weight of your questions,
resounds to your experience.

Hold too the sacred possibility traced by the angels.
The extraordinary within the ordinary,
the voice of the holy in all things.

And so may you, with angels, speak of hope.

PRAYER WORD

with angels, hope

that we would be saved from our enemies and
from the hand of all who hate us

[20] CAVE OF THE HEART

Some calming.
The agitation of early Advent is beginning to recede.
An easing of your fear.

You are rediscovering your stillpoint.
The locus of your belonging.
Place of your belovedness.

The cave of the heart is your true dwelling place.
Here the sense of your union with God deepens.

Place your hand over your heart now.
Return to this stance through the day.

To the ground of your faith, your hope and your love.
Here God dwells.

What – or who – might be born in this humble cave?

PRAYER WORD

here God dwells

that we might serve him without fear,
in holiness and righteousness
before him all our days

[21] THE KICK INSIDE

*And Elizabeth was filled with the Holy Spirit and exclaimed with a loud cry 'Blessed are you among women, and blessed is the fruit of your womb.'**

As Mary was blessed,
so too in the tender mercy of God
are you blessed.

So how will you live today as one blessed?

Let the Christ be carried within you today.
Sense the flutter of life,
the kick inside.

Carry the Christ with love and care.
Be as a mother.
Attentive. Focused. Present.
Do not rush.

You are a home to the holy.

PRAYER WORD

home to the holy

---

* Luke 1

by the tender mercy of our God

[22] THE JESUS PRAYER

You woke long before dawn.
In darkness thick and heavy.
Sleep had left you.
And you found yourself alone
failing to find light in the darkness.

But sometimes the darkness must be given space to be dark.
The wild animals allowed to circle.
Don't fight it. Don't fight them.

Once your senses had become accustomed to the dark,
you went to what you know.

You prayed the Jesus Prayer
Lord Jesus Christ, Son of God, have mercy upon me, a sinner
gradually settling into its rhythm;
slowly finding the prayer carrying all your anxieties;
becoming a means for you to hold others in your prayers;
and forgetting yourself, you entered some serene place.
Lord Jesus Christ, Son of God, have mercy upon me, a sinner

Then a realization.
The dawn from on high that had seemed so far off had broken
upon you.

PRAYER WORD

Jesus

the dawn from on high will break upon us

[23] COME CLOSE

In the holy child
God comes close to us
that we might come close to God.

What might this closeness be like?
Perhaps a *sitting with.*

You know what it is like to sit with one you know and love
for an hour or more.
No words need to be said.

Conscious of each other's presence.
All becomes clear and simple.
Light, love.

Allow God to come close.
Sit.

PRAYER WORD

sit with me

to give light to those who sit in darkness
and in the shadow of death

[24] KEEP VIGIL (CHRISTMAS EVE)

Keep vigil.
Today, tonight.
This Holy night.
And always from now on.

Become as one who awaits with faith, with hope and with love.
However deep the darkness,
you await the Light of the world.

Your sight so accustomed now to night
may discern the faint flickering
of luminescence in the waves
the humble light that can only be seen in darkness.
The light of the world.

The Light that will light your way.

PRAYER WORD

the Light that lights

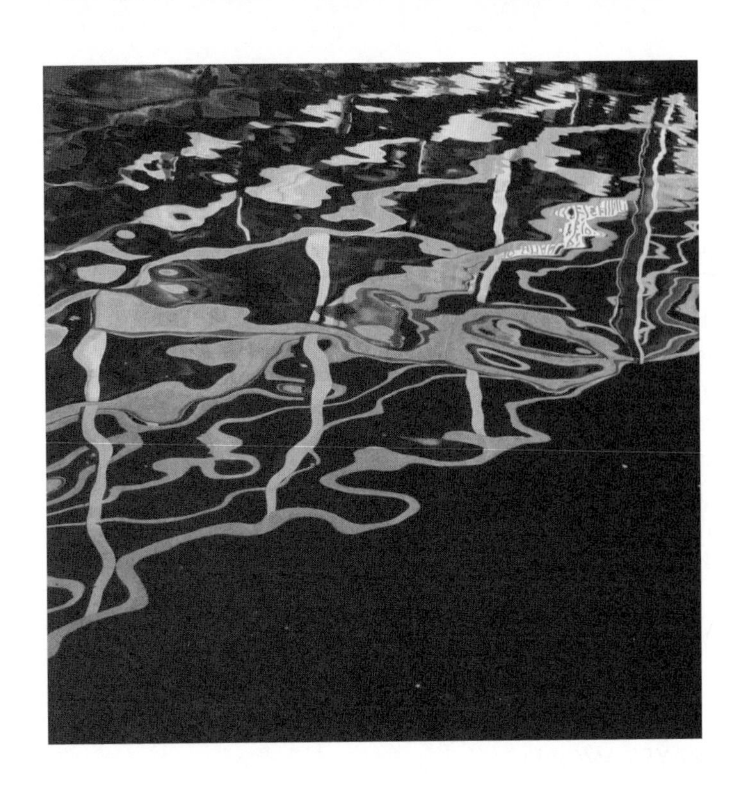

to guide our feet into the way of peace

[25] BORN IN YOU (CHRISTMAS DAY)

Into this world, brutal and brilliant, comes the holy child.

Now let the child trusting and wonderful
be born *in you* –
flooding you with light
so that in the company of countless others
translucent
you may ignite
an aurora of rippling light,
glorious,
a dance of earth and heaven
that will never be extinguished.

May the holy child be born again in you today.

PRAYER WORD

born again in me

glory to God in the highest heaven, and
on earth peace ...

[26] WITH COURAGE AND LOVE (ST STEPHEN)

St Stephen's day.
The first Christian martyr.

You are privileged to have practised the faith
in a time and place in which you have faced no persecution.

Who knows what is to come?
But all you can do is walk the path of the Saviour
here and now,
in the city in which you find yourself,
with courage and with love.

And remember those being persecuted for righteousness' sake
for theirs is the kingdom of heaven.

Live this day with courage and with love.

PRAYER WORD

remember those being persecuted

to you is born this day in the city of David a Saviour,
who is the Messiah, the Lord

[27] SACRED SPACE

A lull.
A quiet day.
A moment to settle into the simple joys of the things that move you.
Books, music, a walk, conversations.
A peaceful sabbath.
A sacred space.

Moments like this,
days like these,
are to be treasured.

Resolve to create more sacred space like this.
To listen, to explore, to allow the spirit of creativity to surface.

This too is the work of heaven,
the glory of God.

PRAYER WORD

this sacred space

glory to God in the highest heaven

[28] SONGS OF INNOCENCE (HOLY INNOCENTS)

Those who would bring destruction and dehumanization to the world
have always corrupted the innocence of the young.

They attempt to extinguish the spark of hope
and the state of peace
into which we are born.

Remember the Holy Innocents.
And resolve this Christmas to do something to restore hope
to the young around you.

That they might again sing songs of innocence
– not from ignorance of reality –
but from a sense that light will always return,
that love is irresistible, and that on earth there may yet be peace.

PRAYER WORD

restore hope

and on earth peace

[29] A NEW INTIMACY

*We declare to you what was from the beginning, what we have heard, what we have seen with our eyes, what we have looked at and touched with our hands, concerning the word of life ...**

What beauty and a vitality in the writing of John.
Born out of personal experience of Jesus.
And of love for him.

Allow the experience of John to open you up
to the possibility of a deeper intimacy
with the Christ.

Peaceful, speak his name. Let him speak yours.

Yet you have never really made peace with your given name.
Could this be a time to do that?
To step into the spirit of St John and St John of the Cross.
John, Johannes, Jonsi, Joni, Joan, Jean, Ieuan, Iain, Ian.

Whatever your name. You are Beloved.

PRAYER WORD

you are Beloved

---

* 1 John 1

Master, now you are dismissing your servant in peace

[30] WORDS AS INCENSE

*Then Simeon blessed them …**

Simeon takes the holy child in his arms.
Anna recognizes the One who comes in such humble form.
As incense in the temple
their words rise as praise,
float in the air as insight
and fall as gift.

The holy family are astonished.
They are blessed.

What if your task today is to see, and to bless?

Truly see those who come your way today.
Look for the light within them.
Bless them.

PRAYER WORD

see, bless

---

* Luke 2

according to your word

[31] ANOINTING THE WORLD (NEW YEAR'S EVE)

*The anointing that you received from him abides in you**

An ending.
Time to look back.
To ask what the year has brought.
And to reflect on what you have brought to the year.

May there be thankfulness for all that has been good.
And healing for all that has been hurt, lost or neglected.
Healing too from all the dehumanizing stuff out there that has at times sapped your will and hope.

You have been blessed – in John's language *anointed* –
in a fragrant healing balm.
So too the world yearns for healing,
for anointing.

This year may you become
some small gift for the world's anointing
wherever you go.
Healing balm.

PRAYER WORD

healing balm

---

* 1 John 2

for my eyes have seen your salvation,
which you have prepared in the presence of all people

[32] IN THE BEGINNING (NEW YEAR'S DAY)

A beginning.
*In the beginning was the Word.**
In the great story as told by John it *all* begins with a Word.
In the silence a sound.
In the darkness a light.

And the new comes into being.
And it continues to come into being!

Allow the Word to be spoken again in you.
In the silence a sound.
In the darkness a light.

Let the Word be voiced.
Let the sound resonate.
Let the light flicker
then burst radiant
in you and from you
lighting the way
that we might see how to shape
a better world for all
here and now.

PRAYER WORD

in the beginning

---

*John 1

a light for revelation to the Gentiles

[33] NORTH STAR

*Abide in him**

Where do you abide?
Where is the point on which you pivot?
The course to which you continually return?

You know that it is your stillpoint,
the place of your belovedness.
Your North Star is the Christ.

The more you look up into the glorious sky
the more natural becomes your sense of your connection
to this North Star.

Study the sky.
Keep on looking up.

Abide in him.

PRAYER WORD

abide in him

---

* 1 John 2

and for glory to your people Israel

[34] WALK THE EARTH

For years, wherever you have been,
you have walked the local landscape each day.

This practice has rooted you into the earth.
Into your setting, reducing your size.
Small footprints.

But also revealing your belonging.
The muddy paths, the heavy seas, the windswept beaches
and the city's streets.
You belong to them all.

Listen again to their wisdom.
To their falling and rising.
Full of goodness
and Godness,
empathy and insight.

PRAYER WORD

falling, rising

this child is destined for the falling and the rising
of many in Israel

[35] STEP OUT

This is the moment, this the day.

You need to commit yourself to a future with no certainties.
To step out onto a road unknown.
Trusting only in the goodness of God,
in the benevolence of the earth beneath your feet,
in the gifts that have come your way,
and in the calling that you sense is yours.

And if on this pilgrimage
you are no more than a sign pointing towards the Love,
this will be enough.

Step out.

PRAYER WORD

in the goodness of God

to be a sign that will be opposed

[36] ALL FLAME

At the beginning of a new phase of life,
what really matters?
What is the *treasure hidden in the field*
worth your everything?

Joni once said – to *go through life with a good heart.*
Jonsi sings to *grow till tall.*
Van *flew into the mystic.*
And the tradition urges to *love God and to love neighbour.*

For the Desert Fathers and Mothers
it is about becoming so transparent,
so full of light,
in the search for God,
it is as if you might become *all flame.*

What really matters to you?

PRAYER WORD

transparent

so that the inner thoughts of many will be revealed

[37] A BURNING (THE EPIPHANY)

The Epiphany.

Jesus the Christ revealed as gift for all.
Light for you.
Light for the world!

Now let the light do its work on you,
making you ever more translucent,
from opaque towards transparent.
Allow the light to shine through you.
And from you – for you too are divine.

This may come at some cost.
And a sword will pierce your own soul too.
The process of discovering our divine nature
is bound to be searing,
a burning, but one in which we will not be consumed.

You are the light of the world.
*Let your light shine.**

PRAYER WORD

shining light

---

* Matthew 5

and a sword will pierce your own soul too

IDEAS FOR REFLECTION AND ACTION

WORKING WITH THE PRAYER WORD

I use Prayer Words as ways back into stillness, helping me to become present, open to the possibility of divine encounter.

1. Allow the Prayer Word to settle quietly within you in time and balance with your breathing, perhaps the first word(s) on the in-breath, the remaining word(s) on the out-breath. Take a brief pause at the end of each in-breath and each out-breath.
2. Let this repeated Prayer Word carry all your yearnings, becoming both your prayer and your resolution.
3. Whenever you recognize your attention wandering (as it will) return to your Prayer Word.
4. When you find yourself able to let go of the Prayer Word and able to be fully present, enjoy the possibility of divine encounter.

WORKING WITH LECTIO DIVINA

1. Read a passage from one of the gospel narratives of the Nativity of Jesus.
2. Notice whatever word or phrase catches your attention.
3. How might the word or phrase that has caught your attention be a gift to you at this time?
4. Pray with the phrase that has caught your attention, allowing it to carry all your hopes and prayers.
5. Let the phrase fall away – enter stillness.

the Prayer Word becoming both your prayer and your resolution

WORKING WITH THE REFLECTIONS IN SOME SMALL HEAVEN

1 Read one of the reflections.

2 What (if anything) in this reflection resonates with your own experience?

3 What surprises you in this reflection?

4 Use the pattern of these reflections here to trace, record and reflect on your own path through winter.

WORKING WITH THE IMAGES

1 Give your attention to one of the images. What feelings does it produce in you?

2 Be curious about the balance of light and darkness in the image.

3 Take a series of photos that explore the relationship between darkness and light in your own setting. Allow them to open up some small heaven each day.

MAKING ART

1 Take a line from one of the Songs of Luke – and in response create a piece of art in your chosen field (painting, music, photography, poem, prose, drama, etc.).

2 Re-imagine an episode from the story of the Nativity of Jesus in your own current context. Create a piece of art drawing on the story and shaped by this setting.

3 In a group setting you could invite each person to choose a different phrase from one of the Songs in Luke's Gospel as inspiration for a piece of work, and then gather the works together for a conversation (or even an exhibition).

explore the relationship between darkness and light